ISIS&OSIRIS

TO THE ENDS OF THE EARTH

AN
EGYPTIAN
M

GRAPHIC UNIVERSE™

STORY BY
JEFF LIMKE

PENCILS AND INKS BY
DAVID WITT

N

LIBYA

ISIS & OSIRIS

TO THE ENDS OF THE EARTH

AN EGYPTIAN MYTH

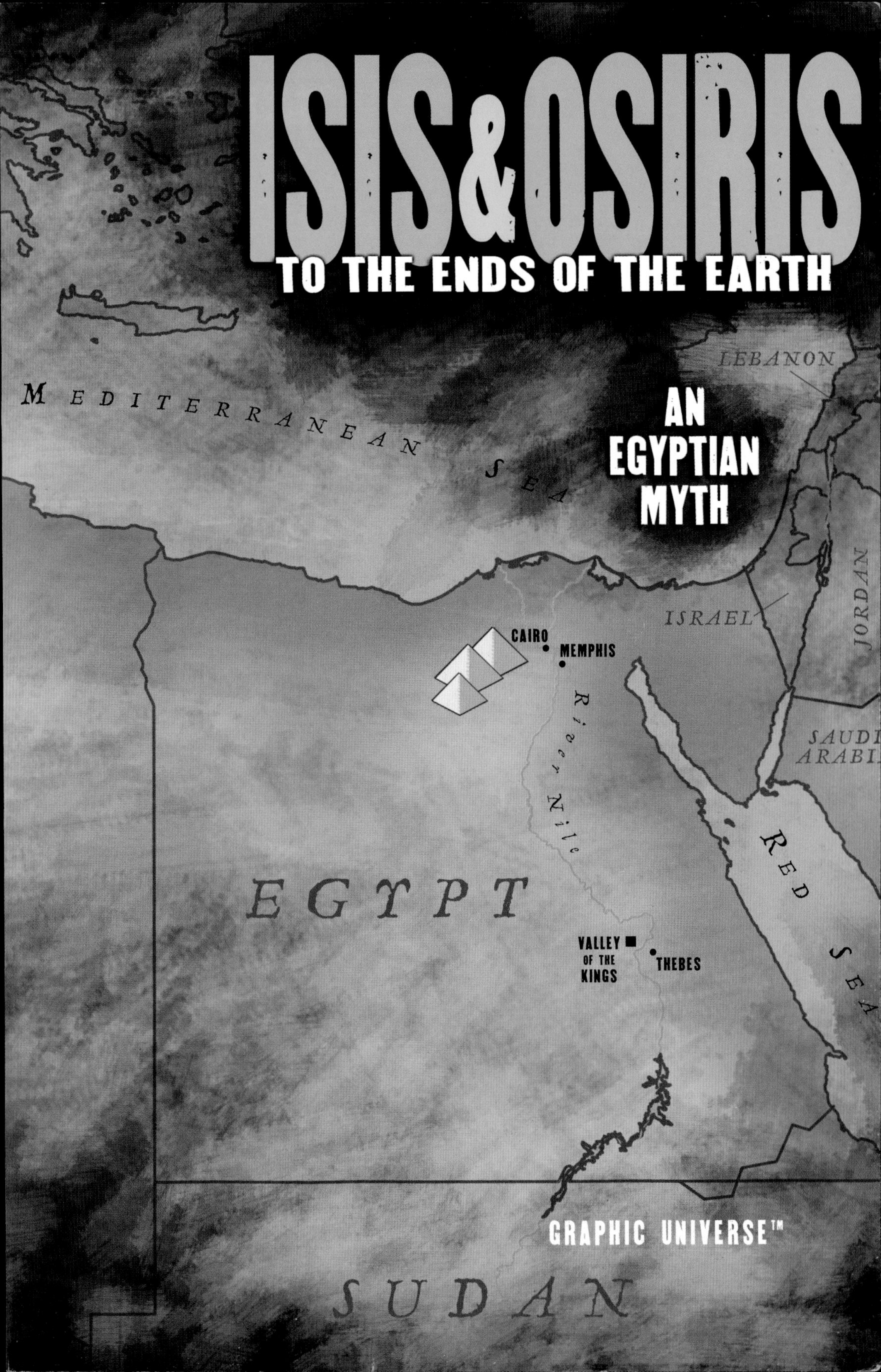

LEBANON

MEDITERRANEAN SEA

JORDAN

ISRAEL

CAIRO • MEMPHIS

SAUDI ARABIA

River Nile

EGYPT

RED SEA

VALLEY OF THE KINGS ■ • THEBES

GRAPHIC UNIVERSE™

SUDAN

THE ANCIENT EGYPTIAN MYTHS THAT TELL OF ISIS, OSIRIS AND OTHER DEITIES DATE BACK MORE THAN FOUR THOUSAND YEARS. AND THE TALES THEMSELVES ARE SET IN EVEN EARLIER TIMES, BEFORE THE RISE OF EGYPT'S GREAT FAMILIES OF PHARAOHS. BUT THESE STORIES ARE ALSO TIMELESS, AS THEY REMAINED CENTRAL TO EGYPTIAN RELIGION AND LIFE FOR MANY CENTURIES. THE IMAGERY USUALLY ASSOCIATED WITH CLASSIC EGYPTIAN MYTHOLOGY IS THAT OF EGYPT'S GLORIOUS DYNASTIES, COMPLETE WITH PYRAMIDS, PHARAOHS AND GRAND ARCHITECTURE. THE ART OF *ISIS & OSIRIS: TO THE ENDS OF THE EARTH* FOLLOWS THAT TRADITION. TO CREATE THE STORY, AUTHOR JEFF LIMKE USED SOURCES INCLUDING *THE MASKS OF GOD: PRIMITIVE MYTHOLOGY* BY JOSEPH CAMPBELL AND *EGYPTIAN LEGENDS AND STORIES* BY ARCHAEOLOGIST MV SETON-WILLIAMS. ARTIST DAVID WITT USED HISTORICAL AND TRADITIONAL SOURCES FROM EGYPTIAN HIEROGLYPHS TO REPRODUCTIONS OF ANCIENT EGYPTIAN ART.

STORY BY JEFF LIMKE

PENCILS AND INKS BY DAVID WITT

COLOURING BY HI-FI DESIGN

LETTERING BY LAURA WESTLUND

This book was first published in the USA in 2007. First published in the UK in 2008 by Lerner Books, Dalton House, 60 Windsor Avenue, London, SW19 2RR

Website address: www.lernerbooks.co.uk

This edition was updated and edited for UK publication by Discovery Books Ltd., Unit 3, 37 Watling Street, Leintwardine, Shropshire, SY7 0LW

British Library Cataloguing in Publication Data

Limke, Jeff
  Isis and Osiris : to the ends of the earth. (Graphic myths and legends series)
    1. Isis (Egyptian deity) - Comic books, strips, etc. - Juvenile fiction 2. Osiris (Egyptian deity) - Comic books, strips, etc. - Juvenile fiction 3. Children's stories - Comic books, strips, etc.
    I. Title II. Witt, David
  741.5

ISBN-13: 978 1 58013 320 3

Printed in China

TABLE OF CONTENTS

THAT'S RIGHT, LITTLE ONE, REST. THE FIRE WILL NOT HARM YOU.

I WILL PROTECT YOU, AND THE POWER OF THE FIRE WILL MAKE YOU STRONGER.

NOW LISTEN AS I SING TO YOU THE SONG OF HOW I, THE *GODDESS ISIS*, CAME TO THIS HEARTH.

LISTEN AND HEAR OF HOW MY HUSBAND, OSIRIS—A GOD AND THE KING OF ALL EGYPT—WAS CRUELLY TRICKED AND OF HOW I SEARCHED FOR HIM.

WE WERE CELEBRATING THE HARVEST MY HUSBAND HAD BROUGHT TO HIS PEOPLE.

THEY LOVE YOU, YOU KNOW.

YOU HAVE BROUGHT THEM SO MUCH AND TAUGHT THEM SO MUCH MORE.

YES, BUT I LOVE *YOU* EVEN MORE THAN BEING THEIR PHARAOH.

ALL WAS WELL WITH THE WORLD UNTIL THE APPEARANCE OF ...

... SET.

MY BROTHER!

DO YOU LIKE THE PARTY I HAVE THROWN FOR YOU, OSIRIS?

THE TORCHES CAN BE SEEN UP AND DOWN THE RIVER NILE.

EVEN THE CROCODILES KEEP THE PEACE TONIGHT IN YOUR HONOUR.

HE *HATED* MY HUSBAND.

I DON'T KNOW WHY. MAYBE BECAUSE THE PEOPLE LOVED HIM MORE. OR MAYBE BECAUSE HE WAS FAVOURED BY THEIR FATHER, GEB.

WELL, THAT IS GOOD. EVEN THE CROCODILES DESERVE A DAY OF PEACE.

NOW COME-EAT, DRINK AND ENJOY THIS FESTIVAL!

I SHOULD HAVE KNOWN, THEN AND THERE, THAT SET WOULD BRING *NOTHING* GOOD...

... BUT HE WAS MY HUSBAND'S BROTHER EVEN IF HE *WAS* JEALOUS.

SO TELL ME, WHAT PRIZE HAVE YOU BROUGHT TO MY PARTY?

DO I SENSE A BIT OF RESTLESSNESS IN MY FAMOUSLY PATIENT BROTHER?

I HAVE A **SURPRISE** FOR THE END OF THE EVENING.

I THOUGHT WE WOULD HAVE A CONTEST FOR EVERYONE HERE.

THE WINNER WILL GET WHAT HE HAS EARNED.

SO, NEPHTHYS, WHAT DO **YOU** THINK OF THIS PRIZE OF YOUR HUSBAND'S?

ME? THIS IS THE FIRST I HAVE SEEN OR HEARD OF IT. I DO NOT EVEN RECOGNIZE IT.

THEN WE **ALL** SHALL LEARN SOMETHING NEW TONIGHT, IT SEEMS.

BUT FOR NOW, LET'S ENJOY THE PARTY!

THROUGHOUT THE NIGHT, WE CELEBRATED. PEOPLE SANG, DANCED AND ATE. THE FRUITS OF THE HARVEST WERE DISPLAYED SO THAT EVERYONE COULD SEE HOW RICHLY OSIRIS REWARDED HIS FOLLOWERS.

THE PARTY CONTINUED ON UNTIL SET'S FINAL CONTEST.

IT IS TIME!

I HAVE HERE THE *BIGGEST* AND *BEST* PRIZE TO END THIS NIGHT.

THE RULES TO WIN IT ARE SIMPLE, BUT THERE CAN BE ONLY *ONE* WINNER.

I HAVE LABOURED FOR MANY HOURS TO PREPARE THIS GIFT. IT IS CARVED FROM SOLID STONE GIVEN BY GEB, OUR FATHER.

IT IS VERY SPECIAL. I HAVE WORKED VERY HARD TO MAKE THIS JUST SO.

I CAN'T *WAIT* TO SEE WHAT HAPPENS.

IT WILL BE *WONDERFUL.*

SO, WHO'S FIRST?

LIKE SHEEP, THEY LINED UP TO TAKE THEIR TURNS, ENTERTAINED AT THE MERE THOUGHT OF WINNING SOMETHING FOR NOTHING MORE THAN BEING BORN THE RIGHT SIZE.

AS I WATCHED, MY STOMACH TURNED WITH DISGUST AT SET'S PRESENCE.

I LOVE HIS WIFE AS A FRIEND, BUT *HIM*...

...HIM, I *HATE*.

I WILL NOT TRY TO FIT. I WILL NOT PLAY HIS GAME.

I *HAVE* TO TAKE MY TURN. IT WOULD BE UNSEEMLY FOR ME NOT TO. I AM THEIR PHARAOH, THEIR RULER AND GOD. IF NO ONE ELSE FITS, THEN THE PRIZE MUST BE FOR ME.

AND GOOD KINGS CANNOT REFUSE GIFTS IN GOOD FAITH.

THAT IS *NOT TRUE*. A KING CAN DO WHAT HE WISHES. THAT'S WHAT MAKES HIM *KING*.

YES, BUT SET IS MY BROTHER AND JEALOUS OF OUR HAPPINESS AS HE MAY BE, HE WILL NOT DO ANYTHING IN FRONT OF THESE PEOPLE.

I WILL BE SAFE.

I WILL BE BACK IN BUT *A MOMENT.*

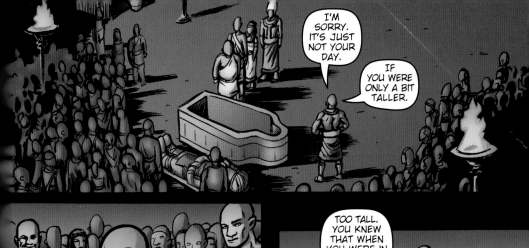

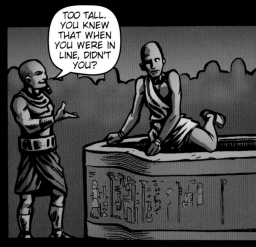

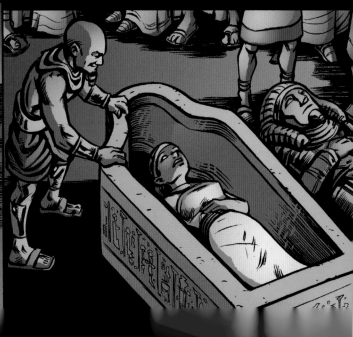

MAY WE NEVER MEET AGAIN.

WHY?!

TELL ME WHY YOU USE YOUR MAGIC LIKE THIS!

ENJOY DEATH, OSIRIS.

MY HUSBAND!

I AM NOW GREATER!

I HAVE PROVEN I SHOULD BE THEIR KING AND GOD!

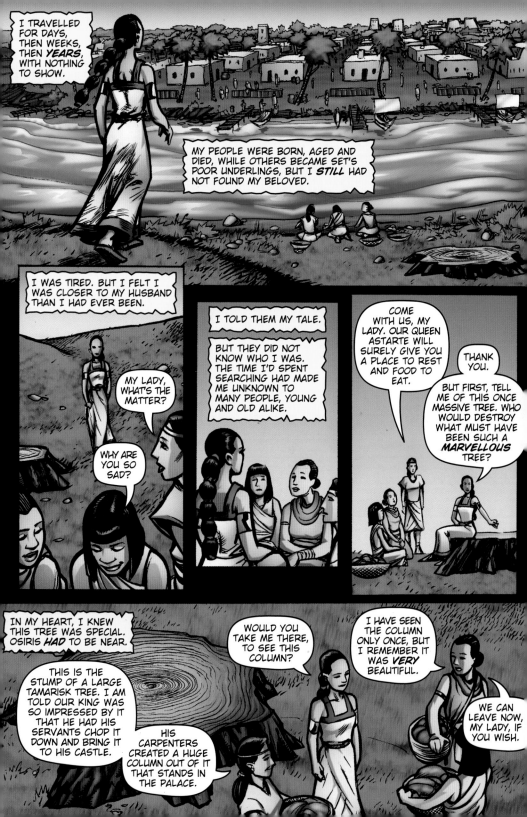

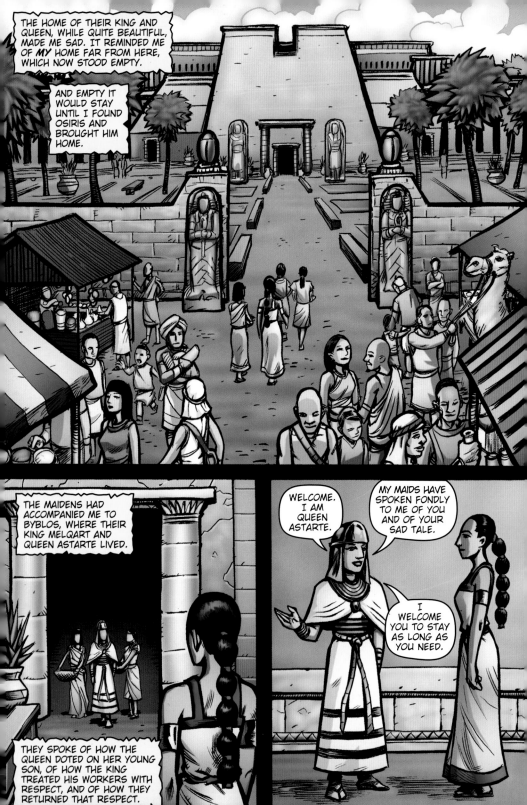

MOTHER...

WHAT?

HE DOESN'T KNOW ANYTHING. YOU CAN LET HIM DOWN.

YOU'RE RIGHT.

I'M SORRY. BUT...

I KNOW. I MISS HIM TOO, AND I HAVEN'T EVEN MET HIM YET.

TO THE ENDS OF THE WORLD

WHO WOULD HATE ME SO MUCH THEY WOULD DO THIS?

YOUR HUSBAND.

SET DID THIS, DIDN'T HE?

I DO NOT KNOW.

MAKING A MUMMY

NOW WE MUST BEGIN THE PROCESS.

WE FOUND ALL OF HIM BUT ONE PART. I'VE INSTRUCTED A POTTER TO CREATE THAT PART FROM THE EARTH THAT OSIRIS HIMSELF HAD BLESSED.

WHEN HIS BODY IS COMPLETE, WE WILL BLESS IT WITH THESE SACRED SALTS AND LET HIM REST FOR A FEW DAYS.

ONCE THE BLESSED SPICES HAVE DONE THEIR MAGIC, WE SHALL BIND HIM TIGHTLY IN LINEN TO SEAL THE ENERGY OF LIFE WITHIN HIM...

...AND HEAL HIM.

IT WOULD SEEM THE DEEDS OF YOUR LIFE WEIGH HEAVILY.

YOU WILL RECEIVE *PUNISHMENT* UNTIL YOU HAVE CLEANSED THE STAIN OF EVIL FROM YOUR HEART.

WHEN YOU HAVE DONE THAT, I WILL WEIGH YOUR HEART AGAIN.

IF IT CARRIES NO HEAVY SINS, YOU WILL RECEIVE THE REWARDS THAT GOOD PEOPLE DESERVE.

NOW, *AWAY!*

YOU ARE NEXT.

COME, LET ME JUDGE YOU.

GLOSSARY

ANUBIS: the son of Nephthys and Set. Anubis has a doglike head and a human body.

HORUS: the son of Isis and Osiris. Horus has a hawk's head and a human body.

ISIS: the most prominent Egyptian goddess and Osiris's wife. Isis is regarded as the goddess of motherhood.

MUMMY: a preserved body. In ancient Egypt, bodies were mummified by removing the main organs and drying the body with a special form of salt. The body was then wrapped in strips of linen.

NEPHTHYS: an Egyptian goddess and Set's wife. In Egyptian myth, Nephthys helps with funeral rites but is also one of the goddesses of childbirth, along with Isis.

OSIRIS: the main Egyptian god, and husband of Isis. Osiris becomes the first mummy and the god of the underworld.

PHARAOH: an ancient Egyptian king

SARCOPHAGUS: an ancient Egyptian coffin

SET: Osiris's brother and the god of chaos and anger. Set is married to Nephthys, and their child is Anubis.

original pencil sketch from page 14

FURTHER READING, WEBSITES AND FILMS

Bailey, Linda and Bill Slavin. *Adventures in Ancient Egypt* (Good Times Travel Agency) A & C Black (Children's Books), 2001. The story of the Blinkerton children's adventures when they travel back in time to ancient Egypt with their guide book from the Good Times Travel Agency. Features a wealth of information about life in the ancient Egypt including clothing, buildings, food and beliefs.

Egyptian Mummies
http://www.si.edu/resource/faq/nmnh/mummies.htm
Learn more about mummification at this site from the Smithsonian Institution.

Encyclopedia Mythica: Egyptian Mythology
http://www.pantheon.org/areas/mythology/africa/egyptian/
This site contains a wealth of detailed information on Isis, Osiris and other Egyptian gods and myths. Browse the articles to get started.

Green, Roger Lancelyn and Heather Corley. *Tales of Ancient Egypt* (Puffin Classics) Puffin Books, 1995. This reissue of a classic collection offers stories of Isis and Osiris, alongside a wide array of other fascinating tales.

Krensky, Stephen. *The Mummy* Lerner Books, 2008. Explore the history and legends surrounding the pop culture version of the mummy.

Parker, Vic. *Ancient Egypt* (Traditional Tales) Chrysalis Children's Books, 2004. Using illustrations this title makes ancient folklore accessible to young readers.

The Mummy. DVD. Directed by Karl Freund. (1932) Universal Pictures UK. Rereleased 2005. This classic film stars Boris Karloff as the mummy. When an archaeologist brings the mummy of an ancient Egyptian prince back to life, mystery and intrigue follow!

CREATING *TO THE ENDS OF THE EARTH*

In creating the story, author Jeff Limke used as one of his main resources *The Masks of God: Primitive Mythology*, by Joseph Campbell, a respected scholar of legends and mythology. Jeff Limke also consulted the book *Egyptian Legends and Stories*, written by the noted British archaeologist and Egyptologist M V Seton-Williams. Artist David Witt used historical and traditional sources to shape the story's visual details—from Egyptian hieroglyphs to reproductions of ancient Egyptian drawings on papyrus (paper made from a River Nile plant). Together, the text and the art bring to life the great stories of ancient Egypt.

INDEX

ABOUT THE AUTHOR AND THE ARTIST

JEFF LIMKE was raised in North Dakota, USA, where he was surrounded by snow, not sand; white-tailed deer, not crocodiles; and wheat fields, not pyramids. There he read, listened to and marvelled at stories from the day he learned to read. He later taught stories for many years, and he has written adaptations of them for slightly fewer years. Some of his stories have been published by Caliber Comics, Arrow Comics and Kenzer and Company. Along the way he got married, and he and his wife had a daughter who loves to read, listen to and marvel at stories.

DAVID WITT (DWITT) is a busy all-purpose illustrator. For three years, he has created flyers, posters, screenprints, comics, T-shirt designs, logos and all variety of illustrations and paintings for the Twin Cities of Minnesota, USA and the world to enjoy.